I0755988

FINISHING LINE PRESS
www.finishinglinepress.com

Diaspora

poems by

Sheri Reda

Finishing Line Press
Georgetown, Kentucky

Diaspora

ISBN 979-8-89990-454-7 First Edition

ACKNOWLEDGMENTS

An earlier version of "Dancing, Twice a Week" was published in *Curbside Splendor.*
"In Praise of Small Miseries" was previously published in *Ecocene Journal of Environmental Humanities* 4.
"Trapped Bird, Locked Door" was previously published in *Examined Life* 8
"Involved" was previously published in *HQ* 34.
"New Bethlehem" and "This" were previously published in *Stubborn.*
"Going Somewhere" was previously published in *Vita Poetica*.

Publisher: Leah Huete de Maines
Editor: Christen Kincaid
Cover Art: © Ridiculous Broomstick
Author Photo: Jeffrey Bivens
Cover Design: Elizabeth Maines McCleavy

Order online: www.finishinglinepress.com
also available on amazon.com

Author inquiries and mail orders:
Finishing Line Press
PO Box 1626
Georgetown, Kentucky 40324
USA

Contents

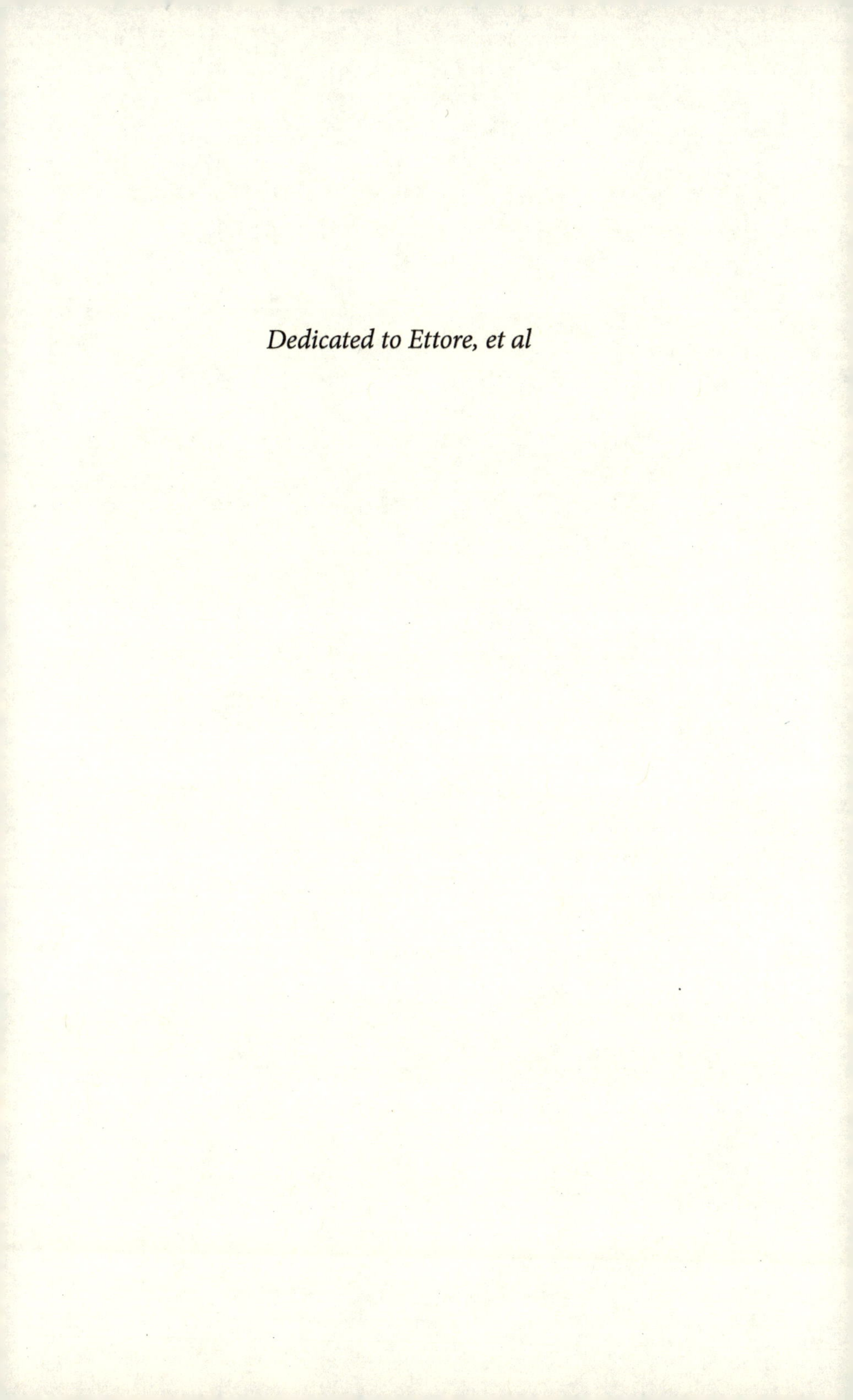

Dedicated to Ettore, et al

Diaspora

The mortgaged sidewalk was just for show: a clean suburban floor
for sneakered feet. Whiteness migrating from the ground up,
blanching our raw belonging. Sundays, we tracked it back in
to the city—past Yellow Grandma's jury-rigged cheerfulness to the
    street
where godforsaken bubblegum gobs metastasized, mingled with tar
on the pavement. Where electric bus wires dissected the sky.
Where red brick chimneys sneezed out storm clouds and smut
settled in our tear ducts. Where a neon spire atop the tavern
with the store in front poked at the gloom and proclaimed the family
name in red and yellow lights every day but Christmas and Easter
because what else would people do and where else could they go
and they might go somewhere else. That door was always open.

Next door, bells gave way to buzzers, and windowless steel
three feet from the gutter faced down rocks spun up from the street
and men spun into despair. Behind the Cyclops door,
a washable plastic walkway dug its yellowed teeth in
to a rainbow-striped rug, heaved itself up three stories,
snaked its way under the painted white panel door
to the railroad flat, made roadways over gold wool carpeting
and gave itself up to one gold couch and two sturdy velvet chairs
encased in crispy plastic—it slurped and bit bare legs.

Back in the kitchen where the wall-to-wall gave way
stood Brown Grandma with the sour smile and the sad eyes
and the cave painting and the picture of Jesus
and six plaster statues of dancing Africans, wild and free
as she was not. And a calendar from St. Peter Canisius, blank.
And a mynah bird who told dirty jokes. Her comforts:
Hard cheese. Homemade salami. Breathy cookies boiled
in gallons of oil and gallons of honey. Sundays, we inhaled
them along with the grit of the factory across the street
and for a moment, life: sweet as the pathless Calabrian hillside.

Here, Now

The breeze feathers my forearm, and I try to remember
something other in the discernible distance between
the pounding sunshine on the sunny side and the soft light over here,
where someone's planted European ginger and those hostas
that bloom and thrive without help or respect.
Something calling me to the reserve my grandpa shared
on our hand-in-hand walks through the hustle of his new country
and mine. Some impervious peace thrumming through
the droneflies subsisting on rot in Calabria and on
to the Italian honeybees imported more than a century ago.
Something humble. Useful. Core to every single one's survival
pulsing through the mid-morning with an invitation
glowing like sour cherry liqueur
in the hosting hands of a burnished nonna.

Benvenuta, she said a lot, and laughed, and motioned for you
to sit. Though the fridge was empty and the cupboard bare
and it was as easy to fall in love with a rich man
as a poor man but no one ever did. She kept laughing,
dimpled arm jiggling as she poured, as she opened
the door to strangers and windows to the wild, as she sautéed
dandelion leaves and mushrooms her husband collected
on his walks along the tracks and served them up
on the table he made for my mother, who gave it to me.
I can't find my way back there. But I can almost hear
their hallway talk in the chattered *chirrup* of sparrows
overhead. I can tack to their scent in the baked-in neighborhoods.
I can loiter in the branches of a lone, lingering elm
beneath the whisk and sweep of these two gray squirrels
chasing one after another after nothing but sunlight.

Garlic Breath

The city is bones and marrow: hard
and taut; it stretches and catches you
quick. When you fall, and you will,
you can gnaw your way through, break it open
and suck out what guts you can find.
Or you can scramble up again
and balance beam across,
tip toe to toe tip:
fibula, femur, ilium, vertebra,
sternum—breastbone—cage of the heart.
Hold your arms out glider-style,
tread gently on the dead.

*

Hiya, she says in suburbanese.
Jus' fine, nods the green-card man.

*

Nonno liked to warn against water: see
what it does to the bottom of boats!
Still his children drank it up and laughed
at the bargains he struck with the merchants
who always saw him coming. After,
Grandma sat him in a rocker, framed
by windows and the afternoon sun. He held
his timepiece to my ear and asked me,
smiling: tick, tick, tick? I nodded,
besotted, in love with this boredom.
Held his hand and he didn't let go,
even after his chair sat empty.

*

What do the too-thin trees in the parkway
whisper through the fall?

*

Great Uncle Mike had feet like a baby's
But once he was just a poor thin wop
who didn't know his stomach from a hole
in his head. Got fixed up with a guy at the Pier,

Got a sweet little job and the fine leather shoes
he kept shined for fifty years. Got to rescue
his pretty little stripper. Got us drinks at the bar
in his River Forest home. Made a career
though his heart wasn't in it, his heart lay broken
and dead at eighteen, stuck in an alley off Rush.
That bar closed down. Mike retired.
Fixed himself another drink.

*

Watch 'em stand there, straight and silent,
saving strength and dropping leaves.

*

Salvatore—Sam—thought he needed his arm,
but County knew better and cut it off.
Gangrene, they said, had staked a claim
in the twelve hours he sat waiting
with the other Dagoes and Pollacks and
the hard wooden chairs and wax-papered snacks
and stubborn, dying trust. He didn't know
English but he knew what it meant
when the doctor took out a rat-toothed saw
and hacked through vein and bone and job.
Who needs a one-armed concrete man?
Sam opened a store. They lived in back.

*

No prairie, no farm, no forest, no wetland,
no romance here in a wilderness clime—

*

Roses in the backyard, chimney stacks up front
and clean, white steam till Sunday comes: back
from college, Mario got mad but Connie shrugged,
When you gotta do what you gotta do:
you dig yourself a plot in cinders and tailings,
grow three sons on bitter greens.
Set yourself firmly into the ground
behind the chain link fence
spliced into the dirt between the tavern
and the grimy shop next door.

Gaze at the trampled ground
and wonder: was ever there wilderness here?

*

This is the place of the stinking
weed. You make do with what you can.

*

Ettore—Albert—bought an old farmhouse
out where Tarzan lost his shoes. They said
he threw chairs when he got mad and they laughed
he always missed. Saturdays, he walked
the rails for mushrooms and dandelion greens
and snails. I don't remember the leather jacket
he saved up to buy me when I was five,
but I recall him teaching me to wave
at the sailors on Navy Pier. Water flowed
over his blue-gray eyes when he pointed
and said, *do you see 'em? Dat's-uh me.*

*

The Ferris wheel at Navy Pier doesn't seem to move.
But don't expect the slowly turning grind to stop for you.

*

I don't want her, you can have her,
she's too fat for me! Theresa laughed and hit him
on the arm: If she lost any weight,
her face would sag. And what did he want,
with all their friends—
you couldn't let 'em eat alone.
Albert chuckled and bent to help her
throw her lovely homemade dough:
yeasty, risen, soft, and warm,
that mound would grow to feed us all,
though we danced endlessly into her kitchen
and pinched off bits of the end.

*

The first day of glory: when you become a bride.
The second day of glory is the day your husband dies.

*

And don't you ever forget to remember Zia
Zizi, who rested her feet on chairs and never
wore no underwear. Crazy Mamie, yelling
out the window at Colomba, Nella,
Hank, and Rose. Lucy with the logy legs.
Gumbas Joe and Mike and Pete.
Mimi, who stepped out hatless once
and met her death of cold.
Nito and Tino—which one of 'em died
from tossing silver coins to kids?
Silver-haired Danny with the good luck chains
who died of the gold shot into his veins.

*

And then the babies: one each for Grandma, Mimi, Mick.
And one for me on Halloween, her name a river reversed.

*

Where did they bury Salvatore's arm?
Where do you think, is my baby? Deep down
in the weedy stink where wild onions rot
and bloom. City of swampland,
bury my bones in your mineral sinkhole;
turn them to stone. I'll rock in the seiches,
gentled by the waves that wear away
my face. And when you're done
kissing me, when you're done slapping me,
when you're done leaving me, turn me to sand.
I tell you now, I want to be
the thing that holds you: lake and land.

*

Lazy Mary will you get up, we need
the sheets for the table. Tra la la ~

* * *

1516 North

All the guys know a guy and all the paisans
remember when and everyone's open secret
threads through the Viagra Triangle, wedged in
the crotch of Old Town and the Gold Coast,
where eyebrows-up Indianans hunker down
with hangers-on still mocking the hippies
who cleared out fifty years ago.
No one's actually played that triangle
since Miss Prentiss with her kind smile and flats
and no time to teach you how to make a
diamond quit to get married. I'm sure you're right
she must've lost her looks by now. Like you.
If she came down here like you she'd have to
buy half a dozen drinks for the Gold Coast
boob jobs just to get a grin, give a thousand
words for no action, even though it's late
Sunday night and the bar's closing
and Tony's smile's gone blank and the hostess
who's usually bland as a preschool teacher
is banging dishes and turning off TVs
and turning up lights and turning locks
and gazing past the bar like a skinny gorilla
picturing life beyond one glass or another.
But kindergarten Miss didn't give a shit
in a different way from the not giving
going on around here. This not
puts the lights out before you're done,
and no remembers you were there.

Olive

We couldn't afford all 64, but we had more than the basics,
including olive, which was an ugly green. Now olive is white
but it used to be a poop color reserved for macaroni boxes,
cannon fodder, and secret internment camps. If you were olive
you rested your head on empty orange juice cans,
taped your bangs straight and sang
the songs of the homeland: *Whistle while you work,*
Hitler is a jerk, Mussolini is a weenie. . . .
Traded Salvatore for Sam, and a job. Surrendered
Ettore for Albert, and a job.
Sacrificed an only-begotten son
for a job. Tucked your life away in foreign-language papers
delivered discreetly to your home.
What's the thinnest book in the world?
The answer: we're lovers, not fighters, you said.
You wouldn't let slip the brokenness
that drove you to where you'd never belong.

We All Fall Down

The one I want is the Kent my mommy smokes on the dyed green
cement patio under my bedroom window
in our treeless new neighborhood.
The dude that sends me tripping across the gym
at my junior year homecoming, choking on an overdose of cool.
A dick with a promise to destroy me slowly. A long, narrow break
outside, propped up against a steel frame in the biting cold,
with stale, white-toothed executives sequestered unknowing indoors.
The joystick I want to suck on: a cowboy billboard slapped up
over an old ad. A fag I want to wave around an endless glamor
and use up utterly, consume with abandon, return to any old time.
The bogey that puts my lips together to blow. The death stick I want
can't be shown on TV. It stinks like an American flag
wound around a corpse. The coffin nail I'm resisting
consecrates my thumb and the first two fingers of my hand.
Is a Buddhist meditation: breathe in poison, breathe out peace.
The jack I crave isn't a gremlin that squats in my throat
recruiting suicide bombers to my esophagus. It's a lucky strike,
a bullet to my chest, residue tumbling out like clouds,
like snow. It hovers like fog, encircles me, a wreath
of eternity, a gloom I wear and shed and hang
out of sight. It's a cool cucumber always out of reach.
A sleek, selective, serotonin-seeking missile.
Slow annihilation. The promise finally kept.

Cacciatore

Same old dawn crawls out from under
the soaked-in scent of chicken soup
and grief: how did they ever and ever
make a feast of this? Drugged
domestic breasts and thighs
chopped and rolled into testicle-sized lumps
set adrift in briny water and
on to the turkey—*I get the neck!*
Ugly aunts gobbling the prickly flesh,
licking their lips, calling the men to the table.
They flashed their ever-sharpened knives
and then handed them over. Helpless, they said.

Training Wheels

Some evenings after I mixed their scotch and water
just right, he took me out to the carnivorous sidewalk
in front of the house, had me mount the second-hand red bike
with the training wheels yanked up, held on to the seat, and ran.
Demanded I chant, *I think I can.* The dream was his.
He made it come true by force of will.
which today we call bullying. He didn't quit
till I could ride a straight line all the way to the corner.
It was up to me to figure out the turns.

Going Somewhere

How do we defend this way we have of birthing
monsters to watch us die? Ants
are not so lonely as us but we disparage them
and yes, I'm speaking for you. I'm not the only one
with shakable faith.
Ants carry on their backs large burdens
and certain purpose, the one enabling the other.
We don't believe in such codependency though
we envy the charming fountains and village squares.
We'll never again depend upon that
pre-Depression bungalow on the Chicago River
or modest mid-century townhouse
squeezed into a side street at the Beaches
or forever-falling-down villa
in the second smallest town in Tuscany.
We can't have what we have and have that
be our lives. Same everywhere. If you attend
the First Congregational Church
in Darien you don't get the liturgy
at Nuestra Señora Del Monte in Cicero
or volunteer time at the Gran Kermes Festival
and raise more money than last year
while the quinceañeras continue
apace
at home
without you.
You can move to Westwood from Chaoyang
or Nikon Town or Tulsa
but you'll never be a native. No one will
ever fully understand why your father
always folded his pants so carefully
before throwing them into the laundry or
why you pause before touching
those metal screen-door handles.
It's true that if fibromyalgia finds you
river blindness probably won't. If
your children are laid open to malaria

they're probably safe from leukemia. None of us get all
the pain though some of us grab most of the money
to steady us on the icy steps to the grand portico
we crave. To be human is not to belong, even if you do join
the army navy air force savings club Burning Man
Davos or one Sundance or another.
To be human is to not belong. To be pierced
by longing. To stagger into thorny unwelcome
in the waning wilderness where you find yourself
target practice for ticks and mere ambience
for ants who hitch a ride on shirtsleeves
where you once thought about wearing your heart.
Those ants are going somewhere while we try not to rot.

2.

The good news: I do and so do you. Rot
like the rest. Crumble to the dirt or dissipate to sky
and birds can pick us clean and shit us back
out to be swallowed whole—ingested, digested,
egested and taken up again, sifted through baleen,
down through esophagus, stomach, other stomach,
final stomach, duodenum, done. Back to the ocean floor.
We needn't be born again, but we all get to die.
The bad news: we don't know this is good news.

3.

An ant can lift twenty times her own sorrows:
admirable to those of us who find our sheets heavy
in the morning, who long to throw them
to the wind. An ant will fight to the death for love
or anyway one last fuck: remarkable
to those of us who undress in the dark. Or never.
We think them armored but they wear their very bones
on the outside. One or two or three or three hundred
thousands may laze while the queen lays
or go home when heavy traffic hits the tunnel
or hang back and let the other ants get the job done.

They know when death takes them someone will
cart them away, as do we cart the fallen
though we sometimes find it difficult to tell who's dead
and who's simply rotting in advance.
We try to do it without help from ants or sea dandelions
or any other reminders of the ways we fall short.
Or long. Or otherwise outside the bounds
of sovereignty—we all want to be queen.
So we hold our kids close and cover their ears with
technologies, and the little monsters are so diverting
we can mine them for years of distractions
before we die and leave only a blown-out husk
and nothing left to nourish anyone or anything.

Close

I collapse akimbo, broken
        stones around the Roman Forum.
You press down upon me:
        the old Italian air.
    We're tight, they say;
        that's nothing new:
there never was enough room for two.
                We simply made do,
          you and I. Funny,
    how as you get older,
   you want a breath of your own.

Tract House

My dad on the midsection of my honored bed
in the big yellow room we sisters shared:
his lively brown hands telling the story
of a prince who sat unvanquished
in a dungeon, a prince
who learned from a spider to try and try again.
Like the ant with the rubber tree plant.
He was a hero, plotting escape
tunnels through basement vats of vinegar.
Back then it seemed efficacious to him
and the other dads to wheedle, threaten, pull the chain
on the closet light, leave us in the dark
with the shadows they left behind,
those dreamtime men who performed
nightmare surgeries
on the poor, sweet stuffed bunny I carried around—
whose empty shell my mother returned to me
when I had kids of my own.

Appian Way

The jest was elusive (we were wolf pups in a basket)
when you tattooed my eight-year-old shoulders
with the heel from one of my patent leather shoes
leaving me with pretty little crescent moons
to mark the moment you'd spun out.
And when I slid expertly under the kitchen table
while contesting your hegemony. Unlike the time
you marched me upstairs, winking, and showed me
how to snap your belt and cry out in phony pain.
And the time I came home late from the movies
to meet your raging fear—*Slap her to the East!*
Slap her to the West! Show the brat that you know best!—
and pressed the damage into my cheekbones
until they glowed yellow and shone blue—
Rah! Rah! Look! See! What my father did to me!
And when I finally said no. And no more. And no again
to the doctors who beat you with science after you died.
And jolted you back when you died again.
And dredged you in science when you died again.
And when I stayed their hands. Took yours.
Placed in the nothing more between us
the confederation we'd always craved.
We (never even knew we) were having fun.

Involved

We're deeply involved,
Like a nice, firm cut
through skin.
Like the quick Colorado
through granite.
Like a vertical
slash through veins.
The path you carve
courses through me
and out
again, taking
more than you notice,
less than you need.

One True Thing

Huddled inside this cave of bones unglowing out, I could use some new skins.
The one I'm in has been pulled too tight too often against the howling.
How do you stay so toasty in there? How do you keep your opiates potent?

At the entryway to the Coliseum a youngish man calls me mother,
asks me to pray for him. I don't know how to explain the dead
don't listen to me anymore. I'm out of sugar, and they won't come near
this place piled high with uncut lemons. I slice some through
to demonstrate intent and they bleed me delicious on spinach, asparagus,
orphaned calves chained with me to the dirt and force-fed strange milk
till the day we need no more. This wins me few friends
but it gets me out now and then, next to other warm meat like me.

He wants me to pretend it's wind, not wolves, nor a huntsman
shuttle-cocking up and down from the formerly ice-capped poles.
Half-hearted promises have left the oven door open. And the freezer door
open. And all the alarms going off at once. One true thing:
we'll stop setting the world ablaze only when there's no more world.

Remedy

Mudpies. Did you ever?
I didn't, but my carrot-orange baby sister
gobbled ashes out of the pewter tray
as if it were a serving bowl
(*it's okay, they contain iron,* said my mom,
at twenty-six, two and a half packs a day,
waving them, careless of the butane in the hair
spray of her Gibson Girl and the paper dress
she bought on Easter back when
she hadn't had cancer yet,
not even once). Still no one played
in mud more than I played at faith,
despite clear indications
of the future crumbling before us.
Maybe everyone feels this way before
grandkids make pessimism too painful
and you learn to pack a bruise with clay,
draw out what toxins you can,
try to save yourself.

Good Ride

Reprising infancy, Senior learns, forgets
and learns, this time about oxygen:
combustible necessity sharp as bleach.
Trained in self-reliance from age six,
when he was commissioned
to empty and clean the imitation brass
spittoons laid out in the tavern every day
but Christmas. And Easter. Believes
in getting up again after they kick you
to the curb. Dedicated to working
for that shiny half dollar resting
at the bottom of the spittoon.
Concludes he did the best he could.
In the nowhere behind his stroke,
he dances, composes, sings, and records
new songs for his one true love.

Dancing, Twice a Week

They don't play the lotto at the U of C. Ask 'em.
They don't like the odds. They don't buy lotto tickets
and they don't work outside jobs and they don't waste time
dancing in bars—the good ones are too far north anyway
but I was talking about smarts: They're too smart
for a lot of things down there. Like luck. They don't need
luck. Have nothing to do with luck. Refuse eye contact,
even, while the rest of us follow the shell game
on the el, let our savings go offshore with us
when we land a one-year contract job in Bermuda.
While we watch our tiny pensions sink into bankruptcy
at the hands of guys who know how to beat a bad bet.
The billboards keep on wheedling, *You gotta play*
to win. But we know we'll lose, and we're in.

Grandma played everyone's birthdays and ages
twice a week. Every single freakin' week
she was off by one or two. Or more. *Oh, well,*
she'd say, *at least we have our health!*
She doesn't say that anymore. These days
she just wishes she was dead, but the nursing home
ladies have told her starving is a terrible way to go,
so now she just she eats her mush and cries.
Sundays, Wednesdays, we visit and avoid noticing
the skin growths and paranoid mutterings and wet bits
of something floating around the edges of her mouth
when she tries to talk. No one pays her any mind
but her imaginary enemy, Jack. And Grandma was right:
she was happy when she had her health
and she didn't have Jack. Cheap joke, sure,

but how else do you talk to the *Wunderkind*
who travel in straight lines with no need for anything
like luck? Who if they want something, get it done
by someone else? Good for them, I guess,
but what I want to know: How do they live
with the clock winding down and not one crazy hope

to hang onto? How do they live and not dance
to the beat of it ticking? They're right about Lotto,
it's a scam, all right—and you can't scam them,
they don't get played. Me, I get played, but
I earned my despair. I'm used to it now
and we're friends, in our way: we visit the grandmas
and moon about luck and go dancing, twice a week.

Tight Quarters

And you all were there. Always
there. In the room. Underfoot.
Stretched out over the crises
that made us a nation
surrounded by warring tribes.
I stepped on you
and you held firm, tripped
and you caught me dangling
over the precipice.
Whirled in circles
and there you were: you
were there. I turned
halfway and you turned too
and we danced and
capital letters fell away—
Today lamented. Tomorrow
promising. Toils
transmuted for kneading,
for chapped hands softened
in the kitchen, for honey
cookies boiling in oil
and the all of us, feasting,
sipping an infusion with no name.

Lemons Lemons Lemonade

You. You're the lemons and the lemonade
(having ripened alongside my own thirst
to squeeze, lick, pucker, suck, swallow). You:
the acid scraping my mouth dry and the juice
running down my chin, messy
and more delicious in memory than moment.
You were very pretty in your flowering
and impossible to consume (as I was
impossible to quench), and I could stay forever
inside the sweet-ish smell of your old plaid jacket
until my eyes begin to burn, and I can't.

Vertigo

I miss our moorings, friends
and acquaintances. I'm sort of with you
bobbing in this this cold vastness,
this opposite sea that sucks up the vertiginous air
where we once pressed together
lifeboat fashion, to keep ourselves afloat
with room for rescues.
I can make out some of your outlines
as I float and wave,
float and forget
to wave, tread water,
thrash around, wait for the boat
that won't come:
We have to save ourselves. Can't shrink
from the germ-ridden grasp of survival.
Personally, I can hold my breath
and struggle repeatedly upward
only a little while longer
but you can do it: find a way
to welcome the cold–water inspiratory gasp.
Suck up the new air and sing.

Times Like These

If you walk nowhere under the dry rain
of an overripe October sky
you can behold the bones
of childhood convictions
you shared with the bronze and silver kids
you knew. You can harken
as distinctly as the last raven calls out
from the tallest leaning tree to its missing mate
the betrayals they suffered and you
can think momentarily perhaps
it wasn't you who lost your way
but faith, too perfect, failed you.
Listen: if a sweeter bird sings you might
send your gaze past the tangle
of bare branches, wonder at the mildness
of this particular fall day, make plans
to mulch hope and grow
something strong as the seasons change.
If silence alone alights, take refuge in the freedom
you still want so badly to surrender
and leap without faith
into the arms of your missing God.
Go where gods go in times like these.

With Thanks

Many thanks to many friends for reading and digesting and commenting on my work—but especially, this time, to my writing partner Ellen Barish and to Mary Corrado, whose clear-eyed, open-hearted readings have helped me clarify and shape dozens of poems.

And to my family, always.

Sheri Reda is an Italian American from Chicago whose "yellow" grandma taught her how to make eggplant parmagiana and whose "brown" grandma gave up on teaching her to make scalille Calabrese. she works as a celebrant, public speaker, and youth librarian. She is the author of *Stubborn*, (Moria Press, 2017) and lead editor of *Life-Cycle Ceremonies: A Handbook for Your Whole Life* (Celebrant Foundation and Institute, 2015).

Sheri's poems have most recently appeared in *Examined Life Journal, Vita Poetica, Locofo Chaps Anti-Trump Anthology* and *Eocene Journal of Environmental Humanities*. They've been anthologized in *The Healer's Burden, The Nature of Our Times,* and the award-winning *Dear Human at the Edge of Time.*

Sheri's literary prose has appeared in *American Book Review, Examined Life, Literate Ape, Oregon Literary Review, Progressive Populist, Still Point Arts Quarterly,* and *Thread* and has been anthologized in *The Healer's Burden*, *Storytellers Stage to Page* and *Storytellers True Stories About Love*. Her memoir entitled *Life is Like That (La Vita É Cosi)* was longlisted for the 2026 International Creative Voices Award.

A Neo-Futurist Emeritus and member of the performance collective Trancesisters, Sheri has performed her work at All She Wrote, Bop Shop, Czar Bar, Essay Fiesta, Fillet of Solo, Funny Haha, The Funny Story Show, Here's the Story, Infinite Wrench, Is This a Thing, Loose Chicks, Reading Under the Influence, The Skald, Story Lab, Soup and Bread, Story Sessions, This Much is True, Too Much Light Makes the Baby Go Blind, Tuesday Funk, and Writer's Theatre Show and Tell.

Sheri has served as Associate Director at Wiggin Library, Editor-in-Chief of *Conscious Choice Journal of Ecology and Natural Living*, Book Review Editor at *Tulsa Studies in Women's Literature*, and Associate Editor at *Cricket* Magazine. She has developed workshops for the Celebrant Foundation and Institute, now known as the Natural Transitions Institute; the Narrative Medicine Institute; the Chicago Conservation Corps; and the CG Jung Center in Evanston, Illinois. The founder of Flow & Moment, LLC, she lives in Chicago with her family and the friendly ghosts of her ancestors.

www.ingramcontent.com/pod-product-compliance
Lightning Source LLC
LaVergne TN
LVHW090540110826
845146LV00003B/1204

* 9 7 9 8 8 9 9 9 0 4 5 4 7 *